THE MISUNDERSTOOD OPOSSUM

WRITTEN BY
MALLORY LAROCCA

ILLUSTRATED BY
EVALIN NADYKTO

First Edition

Copyright ©2025 Mallory LaRocca

Published by Kate Butler Books

www.katebutlerbooks.com

All rights reserved.

ISBN: 978-1-962407-20-5 (Paperback)

No part of this book may be reproduced or transmitted in any form or by any means, electronic or mechanical, including photocopying, recording, or by any information storage and retrieval system—except by a reviewer who may quote brief quotations in a review to be printed in a magazine, newspaper, or on the Web—without permission in writing from the publisher.

This book is dedicated to
my mom, Stacy DeClement,
who always believed in me...
even when I was misunderstood.

Percy was a lonely opossum. He wasn't like the other woodland creatures in Haddon Woods.

The other animals all thought Percy was mean by the way he showed his teeth, and sneaky by the way he rummaged around looking for food.

Percy was subjected to all kinds of mean comments.

"Look, it's that weird opossum, I bet he has ticks!" chattered a squirrel, scampering up a tree.

"He looks spooky with those big eyes and pointy teeth," whispered a rabbit, twitching its nose nervously.

Finn the Fox, usually so friendly, would even judge Percy. "Best not to get too close to an opossum," he said to his little brother. "They're sneaky!"

The other animals didn't understand Percy. Opossums don't have ticks. It was true that Percy showed his teeth, but he was really just trying to be friendly and smile. As for being sneaky, Percy never pulled tricks, but most of the time, he did look for his food under the cover of night.

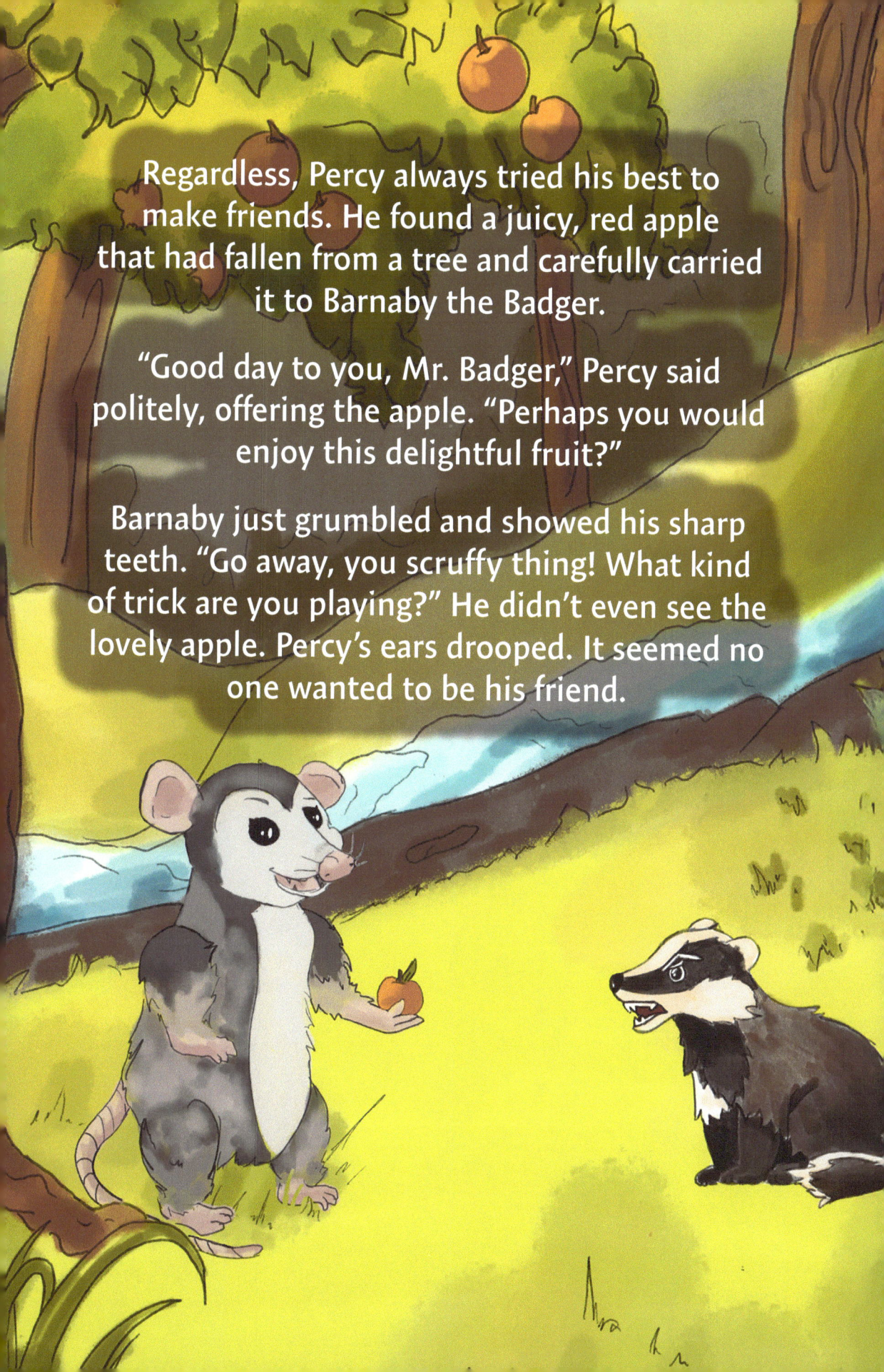

Regardless, Percy always tried his best to make friends. He found a juicy, red apple that had fallen from a tree and carefully carried it to Barnaby the Badger.

"Good day to you, Mr. Badger," Percy said politely, offering the apple. "Perhaps you would enjoy this delightful fruit?"

Barnaby just grumbled and showed his sharp teeth. "Go away, you scruffy thing! What kind of trick are you playing?" He didn't even see the lovely apple. Percy's ears drooped. It seemed no one wanted to be his friend.

One sunny afternoon, a big storm rolled through Haddon Woods. The wind howled, and the rain poured down. Berries were scattered everywhere, and leaves were piled high.

The squirrels couldn't find their buried nuts. The rabbits shivered in their flooded burrows. Finn the Fox worried about his little brother, who had wandered off during the storm.

He then found the shivering rabbits and led them to a dry, sheltered spot under a large fern.
"You'll be safe and warm here," he assured them.

He found little Franklin the Fox huddled under a bush, whimpering. "Are you lost?" Percy asked gently. Franklin nodded, looking scared.

Finn hugged Franklin tightly. "Oh, Franklin! I was so worried!" Then, he turned to Percy, his eyes filled with gratitude. "Percy," he said softly, "Thank you. Thank you for finding him."

The squirrels and rabbits gathered around. They had seen Percy helping everyone.

"You weren't scary at all," said a little squirrel. "You were very brave and kind."

"And so helpful," added a rabbit. "We were wrong about you."

From that day on, Percy wasn't the misunderstood opossum anymore. He was Percy, the perfectly polite and wonderfully helpful opossum of Haddon Woods.

He learned that even though he was different, his kindness could shine brighter than any scary look.

And the other animals learned that you should never judge someone by how they look, but by the goodness in their heart.

DID YOU KNOW?

TURN THE PAGE TO READ
SOME INTERESTING FACTS
ABOUT OPPOSUMS!

Opossums cannot contract rabies—their body temperature is too low.

Opossums love eating ticks! They can eat more than 5,000 ticks in a single season.

Opossums groom themselves much like a house cat does!

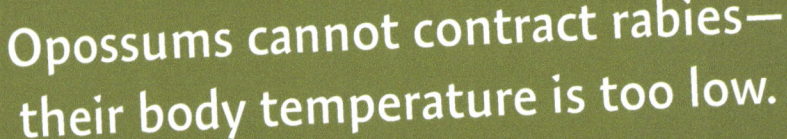

The opossum originated in South America and later spread to North America.

Virginia opossums are North America's only Marsupial

Opossums have 50 teeth!

Just like kangaroos and koalas, opossums carry their babies in their pouch

HOW CAN YOU HELP?

Opossums don't wear shoes,
so garbage can hurt their little feet—
do not litter!

Opossums love over ripe fruit
that have dropped on the ground—
plant a garden with fruits and
vegetables you don't mind sharing

Water is essential for all life forms—
leave out some water, especially
when it is hot

ABOUT THE
AUTHOR AND ILLUSTRATOR

MALLORY LAROCCA is a debut author with a lifelong love for animals and the simple joys of homegrown living. She lives in Haddon Heights, NJ, with her husband, Philip, and their two cats, Finn and Franklin. Mallory spends her free time gardening, cooking, and caring for her backyard bees. Her love of nature and the rhythms of everyday life inspire much of her creative work.

Hello there! My name is Evalin Nadykto! I'm a young illustrator with a passion for detailed, classic-style drawing and illustration that inspired me as a child.

www.ingramcontent.com/pod-product-compliance
Lightning Source LLC
Chambersburg PA
CBHW040032050426
42453CB00002B/89